TIPS FOR FAMILY BUSINESS GROWTH

practical guide for family Business Growth

By

JUDITH WALTER

TABLE OF CONTENTS

CHAPTER THERE
Communication and Conflict Management
- The importance of clear and effective communication within the family and the business
- Developing a conflict resolution process
- Building trust and avoiding conflicts of interest

CHAPTER FOUR
Strategic Planning
- Developing a long-term strategic plan for the business
- Identifying and assessing market opportunities and risks
- Developing contingency plans for unexpected events

CHAPTER FIVE:
Financial Management

- Establishing a financial plan and budget
- Developing sound financial practices
- Monitoring cash flow and profitability

CHAPTER SIX

Human Resources Management
- Attracting and retaining top talent
- Developing an employee handbook
- Providing training and development opportunities

CHAPTER SEVEN

Innovation and Adaptability
- Encouraging creativity and innovation
- Adopting new technologies and methods
- Remaining flexible and adaptable in a changing market

CHAPTER EIGHT
Marketing and Branding
- Creating a strong brand identity
- Developing a marketing plan and executing it effectively
- Leveraging social media and other digital channels

CHAPTER NINE
Customer Relationship Management
- Providing excellent customer service
- Building strong relationships with customers
- Using customer feedback to improve products and services

CHAPTER TEN
Community Involvement and Corporate Social Responsibility
- Contributing to the local community
- Supporting social and environmental causes

- Encouraging employees to volunteer and participate in charitable initiatives

INTRODUCTION

Family businesses have a unique advantage over other types of businesses. They are built on a strong foundation of shared values, a common history, and a sense of kinship that can create a strong sense of purpose and identity. However, establishing a strong family business culture takes more than just having shared genes or a common name. It requires intention, effort, and a willingness to work together towards a common goal.

In this book, we will explore the importance of establishing a strong family business culture and the steps that can be taken to create one. We will examine the benefits of a strong family business culture, such as increased trust, loyalty, and commitment among family members and employees, and how it can help the business thrive in the long run.

Family businesses are unique in that they are built on a foundation of shared values, traditions, and history. This foundation can create a strong sense of purpose and identity for the business, which can be a competitive advantage in the marketplace. However, simply having shared genes or a common name is not enough to create a strong family business culture. It requires intentional effort to develop and maintain a culture that aligns with the family's values and goals.

One of the key challenges in family businesses is managing conflicts that can arise between family members. These conflicts can be related to differences in opinion, power struggles, or personal issues that spill over into the business. By establishing a clear vision and mission statement for the business, all family members can have a common understanding of what the business stands for and what it is trying to achieve. This can help to prevent conflicts from arising or provide a framework for resolving them when they do occur.

Another important aspect of establishing a strong family business culture is building trust and communication. This means creating an environment where family members and employees feel comfortable expressing their opinions, sharing information, and collaborating towards a common goal. Open and transparent communication can help to prevent misunderstandings, build stronger relationships, and foster a sense of accountability among all stakeholders in the business.

Succession planning is another critical component of establishing a strong family business culture. Passing on leadership and ownership to the next generation can be a complex and emotional process, and it requires careful planning to ensure a smooth transition. By developing a succession plan that takes into account the needs and aspirations of all family members, the business can continue to thrive for generations to come.

Finally, sustaining the family business culture over the long term requires ongoing commitment and effort. This means continually adapting the culture to changing circumstances, balancing tradition with innovation, and investing in education and training for family members and employees. By doing so, family businesses can create a culture that supports their success and longevity in the marketplace.

Establishing a strong family business culture is a journey that requires commitment and effort from all family members and employees. By building trust, communication, and a shared vision, family businesses can create a culture that supports their success and longevity. This book provides practical insights and strategies for creating and sustaining a strong family business culture, and we hope it will serve as a valuable resource for family businesses of all sizes and industries.

CHAPTER 1

ESTABLISHING A STRONG FAMILY BUSINESS CULTURE

A strong family business culture is critical for the long-term success of a family-owned business. The culture sets the tone for the overall attitude and behavior of everyone involved in the business, including family members and employees. Establishing a strong culture requires defining the family values, vision, and mission of the business.

The family values, vision, and mission are critical in shaping the direction of the family business. They define what the business stands for and what it aims to achieve. Defining these elements provides clarity and focus for both family members and employees.

1.Defining family values involves identifying the principles that guide the behavior of family members both in and out of the business. These values can include honesty, integrity, respect, teamwork, and innovation. By clearly identifying these values, the family can ensure that everyone is aligned and working towards a common gogoal

2.The vision of the business outlines where the family wants the business to be in the long-term. It describes the aspirations and goals of the family and the business. A well-defined vision statement can provide direction and motivation for the family and employees

3.The mission statement defines the purpose of the business and its reason for existence. It should clearly communicate the business's value proposition and the benefits it provides to its customers. A strong mission statement can help guide decision-making and ensure that the business is focused on its core pupurpose.

4.Creating a positive and collaborative work environment is also crucial for a strong family business culture. This means establishing an open-door policy, encouraging communication and feedback,and treating everyone with respect and fairness. A positive work environment can lead to increased productivity, employee satisfaction, and overall business success.

5.Finally, developing a code of conduct for family members and employees can help ensure that everyone is held to the same standards. The code of conduct should clearly outline expected behaviors and actions, as well as consequences for violating those standards. This can help prevent conflicts and ensure that everyone is working towards the same goals.

In summary, establishing a strong family business culture requires defining family values, vision, and mission, creating a positive work environment, and establishing a code of conduct. These elements help to set the tone for the overall attitude and behavior of everyone involved in the business, which can ultimately contribute to its long-term success.

When it comes to defining family values, it's important to involve all family members in the process. This can help ensure that everyone has a say and feels included in the decision-making process. Once the values have been identified, it's important to communicate them clearly to all family members and employees. This can be done through meetings, memos, or even visual displays around the office or workplace.

A well-defined vision statement should be both inspiring and realistic. It should give family members and employees a clear sense of where the business is headed and what it hopes to achieve in the long-term. The vision statement should also be reviewed periodically to ensure that it remains relevant and aligned with the family's goals.

CHAPTER 2

CLEARLY DEFINING THE ROLES AND RESPONSIBILITIES OF FAMILY MEMBERS

Clearly defining the roles and responsibilities of family members is an essential aspect of maintaining healthy family dynamics. When every family member understands their responsibilities and roles, it can help to prevent conflicts, promote cooperation, and create a more harmonious family environment. In this answer, we'll explain the importance of defining roles and responsibilities within a family, as well as the steps you can take to create clear guidelines for each family member.

IMPORTANCE OF DEFINING ROLES AND RESPONSIBILITIES

Clear communication of roles and responsibilities is crucial for families to function efficiently. Here are some reasons why defining roles and responsibilities is important:

Prevents Conflicts: Defining roles and responsibilities can help to prevent conflicts that may arise due to misunderstandings or assumptions. When everyone understands what they are responsible for, it is less likely that conflicts will occur.

Promotes Cooperation: When everyone knows what is expected of them, it can promote cooperation and a sense of unity within the family. Each member can focus on their area of responsibility, allowing the family as a whole to function more efficiently.

Builds Trust: Clearly defining roles and responsibilities helps to build trust within the family. When everyone knows what they are responsible for and what is expected of them, it can create a sense of accountability and reliability.

Improves Communication: By discussing roles and responsibilities, families can improve their communication. It allows each family member to express their expectations and concerns, leading to more effective communication and understanding.

STEPS FOR DEFINING ROLES AND RESPONSIBILITIES

Here are some steps you can take to define the roles and responsibilities of each family member:

Hold a Family Meeting: Start by holding a family meeting to discuss the roles and responsibilities of each family member. Encourage open communication and allow each person to express their expectations and concerns.

Identify Tasks: Identify the tasks that need to be done regularly and assign them to each family member. This may include household chores, meal preparation, childcare, and other responsibilities.

Consider Individual Skills and Abilities: When assigning tasks, consider the skills and abilities of each family member. Assign tasks that align with each person's strengths, interests, and capabilities.

Be Flexible: Be willing to adjust responsibilities as needed. Family members' schedules and interests may change over time, so be open to discussing and adjusting roles and responsibilities accordingly.

Create a Schedule: Create a schedule or chart that outlines each family member's responsibilities. Post it in a visible location, such as the refrigerator or a bulletin board, so everyone can reference it easily.

Follow Up: Follow up regularly to ensure that everyone is fulfilling their responsibilities. Provide positive feedback and constructive criticism to encourage continued improvement and accountability.

Conclusion
Clearly defining the roles and responsibilities of family members is an important aspect of maintaining a healthy family dynamic. It promotes cooperation, prevents conflicts, builds trust, and improves communication. By holding a family meeting, identifying tasks, considering individual skills and abilities, being flexible, creating a schedule, and following up, you can create clear guidelines for each family member that will help your family function more efficiently and harmoniously.

SEPARATING FAMILY ROLES FROM BUSINESS ROLES

Separating family roles from business roles is essential when running a family-owned business. While it may seem natural to blend these roles, doing so can lead to complications, conflicts, and inefficiencies. In this answer, we'll explain the importance of separating family roles from business roles and provide some tips for achieving this separation.

IMPORTANCE OF SEPARATING FAMILY ROLES FROM BUSINESS ROLES

Separating family roles from business roles is important for several reasons:

Objectivity: Separating family roles from business roles allows for greater objectivity. Family members may have personal biases or emotional attachments that can cloud their judgment when making business decisions. By separating these roles, it can be easier to make decisions based on what's best for the business.

Professionalism: Separating family roles from business roles helps to maintain a professional image. Mixing family and business roles can lead to perceptions of favoritism or nepotism, which can harm the reputation of the business.

Efficiency: Separating family roles from business roles can lead to greater efficiency. When family members have clear roles and responsibilities within the business, it can reduce confusion and ensure that tasks are completed efficiently.

Conflict Resolution: Separating family roles from business roles can help to prevent conflicts. Family conflicts that occur in the business can spill over into personal relationships, which can cause lasting damage. Separating these roles can help to keep personal and business relationships separate.

TIPS FOR ACHIEVING SEPARATION OF FAMILY ROLES AND BUSINESS ROLES

Here are some tips for achieving separation of family roles and business roles:

Define Roles and Responsibilities: Clearly define the roles and responsibilities of family members within the business. This can help to prevent confusion and ensure that everyone knows what is expected of them.

Create an Organizational Chart: Create an organizational chart that outlines the hierarchy of the business. This can help to clarify reporting lines and ensure that everyone knows who they are accountable to.

Establish Clear Policies: Establish clear policies regarding hiring, promotions, and compensation. This can help to prevent perceptions of favoritism or nepotism and ensure that decisions are made objectively.

Hold Regular Meetings: Hold regular meetings with family members to discuss business-related issues. This can help to ensure that everyone is on the same page and that decisions are made collaboratively.

Seek Outside Advice: Consider seeking outside advice from a consultant or mentor who can provide an objective perspective. This can help to identify areas where family roles and business roles may be overlapping and provide solutions for separating them.

Conclusion
Separating family roles from business roles is essential for running a successful family-owned business. It allows for greater objectivity, professionalism, efficiency, and conflict resolution. By defining roles and responsibilities, creating an organizational chart, establishing clear policies, holding regular meetings, and seeking outside advice, family members can achieve separation of family roles and business roles and ensure the success of their business.

DEVELOPING A SUCCESSION PLAN FOR FAMILY MEMBERS

Developing a succession plan for family members is an important aspect of running a family-owned business. A succession plan outlines the process for transferring ownership and leadership of the business from one generation to the next. It helps to ensure the longevity and continuity of the business, and it can also help to prevent conflicts and maintain family harmony. In this answer, we'll explain the importance of developing a succession plan for family members and provide some tips for creating one.

IMPORTANCE OF DEVELOPING A SUCCESSION PLAN FOR FAMILY MEMBERS

Developing a succession plan for family members is important for several reasons:

Continuity: A succession plan helps to ensure the continuity of the business. By identifying and preparing the next generation of leaders, the business can continue to thrive and grow over the long term.

Minimizing Conflicts: A succession plan can help to minimize conflicts within the family. By setting clear expectations and processes for the transfer of ownership and leadership, family members can avoid misunderstandings and disputes.

Financial Planning: A succession plan can help to ensure that the business is transferred in a tax-efficient manner. This can help to minimize the financial burden on the next generation of owners and preserve the value of the business.

Maintaining Family Harmony: A succession plan can help to maintain family harmony. By ensuring that all family members are treated fairly and that their interests are taken into account, the business can continue to be a source of pride and unity for the family.

TIPS FOR CREATING A SUCCESSION PLAN FOR FAMILY MEMBERS

Here are some tips for creating a succession plan for family members:

Start Early: Start planning for succession as early as possible. Ideally, succession planning should begin at least five years before the expected transfer of ownership.

Identify Potential Successors: Identify potential successors within the family. This should be based on factors such as their skills, experience, and interest in the business.

Determine Roles and Responsibilities: Determine the roles and responsibilities of each family member within the business. This should be based on their skills and experience, and should be agreed upon by all family members.

Create a Timeline: Create a timeline for the transfer of ownership and leadership. This should include milestones such as training, mentoring, and the transfer of shares.

Get Professional Advice: Seek professional advice from lawyers, accountants, and business advisors. They can provide guidance on legal, tax, and financial issues related to succession planning.

Communicate with Family Members: Communicate with all family members about the succession plan. This should include regular updates on the progress of the plan, as well as opportunities for feedback and input.

CONCLUSION

Developing a succession plan for family members is an important aspect of running a family-owned business. It helps to ensure continuity, minimize conflicts, plan for financial issues, and maintain family harmony. By starting early, identifying potential successors, determining roles and responsibilities, creating a timeline, seeking professional advice, and communicating with family members, you can create a succession plan that works for your family and your business.

CHAPTER THREE

COMMUNICATION AND CONFLICT MANAGEMENT

Communication and conflict management are essential components of running a successful family-owned business. Effective communication helps to promote understanding and collaboration, while conflict management helps to resolve disagreements and maintain family harmony. In this answer, we'll explain the importance of communication and conflict management in a family business and provide some tips for improving them.

IMPORTANCE OF COMMUNICATION IN A FAMILY BUSINESS

Effective communication is essential in a family-owned business for several reasons:

Clarity: Clear communication helps to ensure that everyone understands their roles and responsibilities. This helps to avoid misunderstandings and confusion.

Collaboration: Effective communication promotes collaboration and teamwork. It allows family members to work together towards common goals.

Trust: Good communication helps to build trust within the family. When everyone is open and transparent with each other, it helps to foster a sense of trust and mutual respect.

Innovation: Open communication encourages innovation and creativity. It allows family members to share their ideas and perspectives, leading to new and innovative solutions.

TIPS FOR IMPROVING COMMUNICATION IN A FAMILY BUSINESS

Here are some tips for improving communication in a family-owned business:

Regular Meetings: Schedule regular meetings to discuss business matters. This helps to ensure that everyone is on the same page and has a chance to share their thoughts and ideas.

Listen: Listen to each other and show respect for differing opinions. Encourage open and honest communication.

Communicate Clearly: Be clear and concise when communicating. Avoid vague language and be specific about expectations and goals.

Use Multiple Channels: Use multiple channels of communication, such as email, phone, and face-to-face meetings. This ensures that everyone is kept informed, regardless of their location or availability.

Importance of Conflict Management in a Family Business

Conflict is inevitable in any organization, but in a family-owned business, it can be particularly challenging. Conflict management is important for several reasons:

Maintaining Family Harmony: Effective conflict management helps to maintain family harmony. It helps to resolve disagreements and prevent them from escalating into larger conflicts.

Improved Decision Making: Conflict can actually be beneficial in a family-owned business, as it can lead to better decision making. By encouraging different viewpoints, it helps to ensure that all options are considered before making a decision.

Business Growth: Effective conflict management can help to foster innovation and business growth. It encourages family members to think creatively and work together towards common goals.

TIPS FOR EFFECTIVE CONFLICT MANAGEMENT IN A FAMILY BUSINESS

Here are some tips for effective conflict management in a family-owned business:

Address Conflicts Early: Address conflicts as soon as they arise. This helps to prevent them from escalating and becoming more difficult to resolve.

Remain Objective: Remain objective and focus on the issue at hand. Avoid making personal attacks or getting emotional.

Find Common Ground: Look for areas of agreement and find common ground. This can help to reduce tensions and promote collaboration.

Seek Help: If conflicts are particularly difficult to resolve, seek the help of a mediator or outside advisor. They can provide an impartial perspective and help to find a resolution that works for everyone.

Conclusion

Effective communication and conflict management are essential components of running a successful family-owned business. By improving communication, family members can promote understanding, collaboration, trust, and innovation. By practicing effective conflict management, family members can maintain family harmony, improve decision making, and foster business growth. By following the tips outlined above, family businesses can build a strong foundation for success.

The importance of clear and effective communication within the family and the business

Clear and effective communication is crucial in any business, but it becomes even more critical in a family-owned business. Family businesses have unique dynamics, with personal relationships and emotions intertwined with business decisions. As such, clear and effective communication is essential to ensure that everyone is on the same page, that misunderstandings are avoided, and that conflicts are resolved promptly.

Here are some reasons why clear and effective communication is so important in a family-owned business:

Builds Trust: Good communication builds trust among family members. When everyone communicates openly and transparently, it fosters a sense of trust and mutual respect.

Avoids Misunderstandings: Family businesses can be complex, and there is often a lot at stake. Clear and effective communication helps to avoid misunderstandings, which can have serious consequences.

Encourages Collaboration: Effective communication encourages collaboration and teamwork. Family members can work together towards common goals and share their ideas and perspectives, leading to new and innovative solutions.

Increases Efficiency: Clear communication ensures that everyone understands their roles and responsibilities. It helps to avoid duplication of effort, missed deadlines, and other inefficiencies.

Improves Decision Making: Effective communication promotes better decision making. When family members communicate openly and honestly, it ensures that all viewpoints are considered before making a decision.

Promotes Accountability: Clear communication promotes accountability. When everyone understands their roles and responsibilities, it ensures that they are held accountable for their actions.

TIPS FOR CLEAR AND EFFECTIVE COMMUNICATION IN A FAMILY-OWNED BUSINESS

Schedule Regular Meetings: Schedule regular meetings to discuss business matters. This helps to ensure that everyone is on the same page and has a chance to share their thoughts and ideas.

Listen: Listen to each other and show respect for differing opinions. Encourage open and honest communication.

Communicate Clearly: Be clear and concise when communicating. Avoid vague language and be specific about expectations and goals.

Use Multiple Channels: Use multiple channels of communication, such as email, phone, and face-to-face meetings. This ensures that everyone is kept informed, regardless of their location or availability.

Use Written Communication: Written communication, such as memos, emails, or texts, can be particularly useful in a family-owned business. It helps to ensure that everyone has a clear understanding of expectations and goals.

In conclusion, clear and effective communication is essential in a family-owned business. It builds trust, avoids misunderstandings, encourages collaboration, increases efficiency, improves decision making, and promotes accountability. By following the tips outlined above, family-owned businesses can ensure that they communicate clearly and effectively, leading to greater success and harmony in the long run.

Developing A Conflict Resolution Process

Conflict is a natural part of any organization, including family-owned businesses. In a family-owned business, conflicts can be particularly challenging as personal relationships and emotions are often intertwined with business decisions. However, conflicts left unresolved can have serious consequences, including a breakdown in communication, damaged relationships, and even the failure of the business. Therefore, it is crucial to develop a conflict resolution process to manage conflicts effectively.

HERE ARE SOME STEPS TO DEVELOP A CONFLICT RESOLUTION PROCESS

Define the problem: The first step in resolving a conflict is to define the problem. Identify the specific issue or issues causing the conflict.

Identify the parties involved: Identify the parties involved in the conflict. This may include family members, employees, or other stakeholders.

Gather information: Collect all relevant information about the conflict, including facts, opinions, and perspectives.

Establish ground rules: Establish ground rules for the conflict resolution process. These may include guidelines for behavior, such as respecting each other's opinions, avoiding personal attacks, and actively listening.

Identify possible solutions: Identify possible solutions to the conflict. Brainstorm a range of options and evaluate their feasibility.

Evaluate options: Evaluate each option against a set of criteria, such as feasibility, cost, and impact on the business.

Select a solution: Select a solution that is mutually acceptable to all parties involved.

Implement the solution: Implement the chosen solution and monitor its effectiveness.

Review the process: Review the conflict resolution process regularly to ensure that it remains effective and relevant.

Tips for Effective Conflict Resolution in Family-Owned Businesses:

Address conflicts promptly: Address conflicts promptly before they escalate.

Remain objective: Try to remain objective when dealing with conflicts, even when emotions are high.

Encourage open communication: Encourage open communication and active listening to ensure that everyone's perspective is heard.

Focus on the problem, not the person: Focus on the problem, not the person, to avoid personal attacks.

Use a mediator: Consider using a mediator to help resolve conflicts impartially.

Keep emotions in check: Try to keep emotions in check during the conflict resolution process.

In conclusion, developing a conflict resolution process is essential for managing conflicts effectively in family-owned businesses. By following the steps outlined above and implementing the tips for effective conflict resolution, family-owned businesses can resolve conflicts promptly and avoid negative consequences such as a breakdown in communication, damaged relationships, and business failure.

BUILDING TRUST AND AVOIDING CONFLICTS OF INTEREST

Building trust and avoiding conflicts of interest are crucial for the success of any business, and particularly important in a family-owned business. Family-owned businesses often involve close relationships between family members, which can create potential conflicts of interest. Therefore, it is essential to build trust among family members and establish clear guidelines for avoiding conflicts of interest.

Here are some ways to build trust and avoid conflicts of interest in a family-owned business:

Separate personal and business finances: Separate personal and business finances to avoid conflicts of interest. This helps to ensure that family members are not making decisions based on personal gain rather than the best interests of the business.

Establish clear guidelines: Establish clear guidelines for how decisions are made, who has decision-making authority, and what constitutes a conflict of interest.

Communicate openly: Communicate openly and honestly with family members. This helps to build trust and ensure that everyone is on the same page.

Keep family issues separate: Keep family issues separate from business issues. Avoid bringing personal issues into the workplace.

Set clear expectations: Set clear expectations for family members who work in the business. This includes establishing clear job descriptions, performance metrics, and promotion criteria.

Reward based on merit: Reward family members based on merit rather than family status. This helps to ensure that everyone is held to the same standards and promotes a culture of fairness.

Use third-party advisors: Use third-party advisors, such as accountants and lawyers, to provide objective advice and help manage conflicts of interest.

Establish a code of conduct: Establish a code of conduct that outlines ethical standards and expectations for behavior. This helps to ensure that everyone is on the same page and promotes a culture of integrity.

In conclusion, building trust and avoiding conflicts of interest are crucial for the success of a family-owned business. By separating personal and business finances, establishing clear guidelines, communicating openly, keeping family issues separate, setting clear expectations, rewarding based on merit, using third-party advisors, and establishing a code of conduct, family-owned businesses can build trust and promote a culture of integrity. This helps to ensure that family-owned businesses remain successful, sustainable, and harmonious over the long term.

CHAPTER FOUR

DEVELOPING A LONG-TERM STRATEGIC PLAN FOR THE BUSINESS

Developing a long-term strategic plan for a business is a critical process that involves identifying the business's goals, developing a roadmap to achieve them, and assessing potential risks and opportunities in the market. This plan helps businesses to focus their efforts, allocate resources effectively, and make informed decisions that can lead to sustainable growth and success. Here are the steps involved in developing a long-term strategic plan and identifying and assessing market opportunities and risks:

Step 1: Conduct a SWOT Analysis

The first step in developing a long-term strategic plan is to conduct a SWOT analysis. SWOT stands for Strengths, Weaknesses, Opportunities, and Threats. This analysis helps businesses to understand their internal and external environment and identify areas where they can improve or capitalize on opportunities. The SWOT analysis includes:

Strengths: These are the positive attributes of the business, such as a strong brand reputation, a talented workforce, or proprietary technology.
Weaknesses: These are the areas where the business needs improvement, such as inefficient processes, low employee morale, or limited resources.
Opportunities: These are the potential areas of growth or new markets that the business can explore, such as emerging technologies, changing customer needs, or expanding into new geographies.
Threats: These are the external factors that can affect the business's performance, such as

economic downturns, new competitors, or changing regulations.

Step 2: Set Long-Term Goals
After conducting a SWOT analysis, the next step is to set long-term goals. These goals should be specific, measurable, attainable, relevant, and time-bound (SMART). They should be aligned with the business's mission and vision and should guide the business's actions and decisions. Examples of long-term goals include:

Increasing revenue by a certain percentage over the next five years
Expanding into new markets or geographies
Developing new products or services to meet changing customer needs
Improving employee retention and engagement
Enhancing the brand reputation through effective marketing and public relations efforts.
Step 3: Identify Market Opportunities

The next step is to identify market opportunities. This involves analyzing trends and patterns in the market, studying customer behavior, and researching the competition. Businesses can also leverage data analytics tools to gather insights about their customers and the market. Some strategies to identify market opportunities include:

Conducting market research to understand customer needs and preferences
Analyzing industry trends and identifying emerging technologies
Monitoring social media and online reviews to understand customer sentiment
Studying the competition and identifying areas where the business can differentiate itself.
Step 4: Assess Market Risks

Along with identifying market opportunities, businesses should also assess market risks. This involves analyzing potential threats to the business, such as new competitors, changing regulations, and economic downturns.
Businesses should develop contingency plans to mitigate these risks and ensure they are prepared

for any potential disruptions. Strategies to assess market risks include:

Conducting a PEST analysis to understand the political, economic, social, and technological factors that can affect the business
Analyzing the competition and identifying potential threats and weaknesses
Monitoring regulatory changes and assessing the impact on the business
Developing contingency plans to mitigate potential risks.
Step 5: Develop a Roadmap

Finally, businesses should develop a roadmap to achieve their long-term goals. This roadmap should include specific actions and strategies to capitalize on market opportunities and mitigate market risks. It should also outline key performance indicators and metrics to track progress towards achieving long-term goals. Strategies to develop a roadmap include:

Creating a timeline that outlines specific milestones and deadlines
Assigning responsibilities and roles to team members
Allocating resources effectively to achieve goals
Establishing metrics and KPIs to track progress and adjust strategies as needed.

In conclusion, developing a long-term strategic plan for a business is a critical process that requires careful analysis, planning, and execution. By conducting a SWOT analysis, setting long-term goals, identifying market opportunities, and assessing market risks, businesses can develop a roadmap to achieve sustainable growth and success. The strategic plan should guide the business's actions and decisions and should be reviewed and adjusted regularly to ensure it remains relevant and effective. With a well-developed strategic plan, businesses can allocate resources effectively, capitalize on market opportunities, and mitigate potential risks, leading to long-term success and profitability.

DEVELOPING CONTINGENCY PLANS FOR UNEXPECTED EVENTS

Developing contingency plans for unexpected events is an essential part of business planning. Contingency planning involves identifying potential risks and developing strategies to mitigate their impact on the business. The goal is to ensure that the business can continue to operate effectively in the event of unexpected disruptions. Here are the steps involved in developing contingency plans for unexpected events:

Step 1: Identify Potential Risks

The first step in developing a contingency plan is to identify potential risks. These can include natural disasters, cybersecurity breaches, supply chain disruptions, or unexpected changes in the economy or regulatory environment. The key is to identify the risks that are most likely to affect the business and have the most significant impact.

Step 2: Assess the Impact of the Risks

Once potential risks are identified, the next step is to assess their potential impact on the business. This involves evaluating the likelihood of each risk occurring and the potential consequences for the business. For example, a natural disaster could result in damage to the physical location of the business, loss of data or inventory, or interruption of operations.

Step 3: Develop Strategies to Mitigate Risks

Based on the assessment of potential risks, the next step is to develop strategies to mitigate their impact on the business. These strategies can include:

Developing backup plans for critical business functions or processes

Ensuring that data is backed up and can be restored quickly in the event of a cybersecurity breach or other data loss
Diversifying suppliers to reduce the impact of supply chain disruptions
Maintaining adequate insurance coverage to protect against financial losses
Developing communication plans to keep employees, customers, and other stakeholders informed in the event of an unexpected event.
Step 4: Test and Update the Contingency Plan

Once a contingency plan is developed, it is essential to test it to ensure it is effective. This can involve conducting tabletop exercises or simulations to evaluate the plan's effectiveness in a controlled environment. It is also important to regularly review and update the plan to reflect changes in the business environment or new risks that may emerge.

Step 5: Communicate the Contingency Plan

Finally, it is essential to communicate the contingency plan to all stakeholders, including employees, customers, and suppliers. This helps ensure that everyone is aware of the plan and understands their role in executing it. Communication can include training sessions, written materials, or online resources that provide information on the plan and how it will be implemented.

In conclusion, developing contingency plans for unexpected events is critical to ensuring business continuity and minimizing the impact of disruptions. By identifying potential risks, assessing their impact, developing strategies to mitigate their effects, testing and updating the plan, and communicating it to all stakeholders, businesses can be better prepared to handle unexpected events and maintain operations during times of uncertainty.

CHAPTER FIVE

ESTABLISHING A FINANCIAL PLAN AND BUDGET

Establishing a financial plan and budget is an essential part of running a successful business. A financial plan outlines a company's financial goals and strategies for achieving them, while a budget provides a detailed overview of expected income and expenses over a specific period. Here are the steps involved in establishing a financial plan and budget for a business:

Step 1: Determine Financial Goals

The first step in developing a financial plan is to determine the company's financial goals. This can include increasing revenue, reducing expenses, improving profitability, or achieving specific financial ratios such as debt-to-equity or return on investment (ROI). Goals should be specific, measurable, achievable, relevant, and time-bound (SMART).

Step 2: Assess Financial Health

The next step is to assess the company's financial health by analyzing financial statements such as the balance sheet, income statement, and cash flow statement. This helps to identify areas of strength and weakness, such as high debt levels, low profit margins, or inconsistent cash flow.

Step 3: Develop Financial Strategies

Based on the assessment of the company's financial health and goals, the next step is to develop financial strategies. These can include strategies for increasing revenue, reducing expenses, improving cash flow, or managing debt. Strategies should be tailored to the company's specific situation and goals.

Step 4: Create a Budget

Once financial goals and strategies are established, the next step is to create a budget. A budget is a detailed plan that outlines expected income and expenses over a specific period, typically a year. The budget should include revenue projections, expense categories such as salaries, rent, and utilities, and a cash flow forecast.

Step 5: Monitor Performance

The final step is to monitor financial performance regularly to ensure that the company is on track to achieve its financial goals. This can involve comparing actual financial results to the budget, identifying variances, and taking corrective action as needed. It is also important to adjust the financial plan and budget as needed based on changes in the business environment or unexpected events.

In conclusion, establishing a financial plan and budget is critical to the success of any business.

By determining financial goals, assessing financial health, developing financial strategies, creating a budget, and monitoring performance, businesses can make informed financial decisions and achieve long-term financial success. A well-planned and executed financial plan and budget can also provide a framework for growth and help businesses to manage risk effectively.

Developing Sound Financial Practices

Developing sound financial practices is essential for achieving financial stability and security in the long run. It involves creating a budget, managing debt, building an emergency fund, saving for retirement, and investing wisely. In this article, we will discuss each of these practices in detail.

Create a Budget:
Creating a budget is the first step in developing sound financial practices. It involves tracking your income and expenses and creating a plan

for spending and saving your money. To create a budget, start by listing all of your sources of income, including your salary, rental income, and any other sources of income. Next, list all of your monthly expenses, including rent or mortgage, utilities, groceries, transportation, and entertainment. Once you have a clear picture of your income and expenses, you can create a plan for how much money you will allocate to each expense category. A budget will help you prioritize your spending, avoid overspending, and ensure that you are saving enough for your financial goals.

Manage Debt:
Managing debt is an important part of sound financial practices. High-interest debt, such as credit card debt, can quickly become unmanageable and lead to financial distress. To manage your debt, start by creating a plan to pay off your debts as quickly as possible. This may involve consolidating your debts into a single loan with a lower interest rate or making extra payments on your highest interest debts first.

Additionally, avoid taking on new debts unless it is absolutely necessary.

Build an Emergency Fund:
Building an emergency fund is another important financial practice. An emergency fund is a savings account that you can use to cover unexpected expenses, such as medical bills or car repairs. Ideally, your emergency fund should be able to cover three to six months' worth of living expenses. To build an emergency fund, start by setting aside a small amount of money each month until you have built up enough savings.

Save for Retirement:
Saving for retirement is essential to ensure that you have enough money to support yourself in your later years. To save for retirement, start by contributing to a retirement savings account, such as a 401(k) or IRA. These accounts offer tax benefits and can help your money grow over time. Additionally, consider increasing your

contributions over time to ensure that you are saving enough for retirement.

Invest Wisely:
Investing wisely is another important financial practice. Investing can help your money grow over time and can help you achieve your long-term financial goals. To invest wisely, start by understanding your investment options and the associated risks. Consider working with a financial advisor to develop an investment plan that aligns with your financial goals and risk tolerance.

In summary, developing sound financial practices involves creating a budget, managing debt, building an emergency fund, saving for retirement, and investing wisely. These practices can help you achieve financial stability and security over the long run.

Monitoring Cash Flow And Profitability

Monitoring cash flow and profitability is crucial for the success of any business, regardless of its size or industry. Cash flow refers to the movement of cash in and out of a business, while profitability refers to the amount of profit a business earns over a given period. In this article, we will discuss why monitoring cash flow and profitability is important and how businesses can do it effectively.

Why Monitor Cash Flow and Profitability?

Monitoring cash flow and profitability is important for several reasons:

Cash flow management: A business needs to have a positive cash flow to pay its bills and invest in growth. Monitoring cash flow can help businesses identify any potential cash flow problems early and take corrective action.

Financial planning: Knowing how much money is coming in and going out of the business can help businesses plan their expenses and investments better.

Debt management: A business that has a positive cash flow is better positioned to manage its debt and pay off loans on time.

Decision making: Monitoring cash flow and profitability can help businesses make informed decisions about investments, expenses, and pricing strategies.

How to Monitor Cash Flow and Profitability?

Use accounting software: Accounting software, such as QuickBooks or Xero, can help businesses track cash flow and profitability easily. These tools can generate reports that show cash inflows and outflows, revenue, expenses, and profitability.

Create a cash flow statement: A cash flow statement shows the movement of cash in and out of a business over a period. It can help businesses identify areas where cash is being tied up and take corrective action.

Analyze profitability: Businesses can calculate profitability by subtracting expenses from revenue. Profitability can be monitored using financial ratios, such as gross margin or net profit margin, to measure the efficiency of the business operations.

Set financial goals: Setting financial goals can help businesses monitor cash flow and profitability effectively. Goals can include increasing revenue, reducing expenses, or improving profit margins.

Conduct regular reviews: Monitoring cash flow and profitability should be done regularly, such as monthly or quarterly. Regular reviews can help businesses identify trends and take corrective action if necessary.

In conclusion, monitoring cash flow and profitability is crucial for the success of any business. By using accounting software, creating a cash flow statement, analyzing profitability, setting financial goals, and conducting regular reviews, businesses can monitor their financial performance effectively and make informed decisions about their operat

CHAPTER SIX

HUMAN RESOURCES MANAGEMENT

Human resources management (HRM) is the process of managing an organization's employees to achieve its goals and objectives. HRM involves recruiting, training, and developing employees, administering employee benefits and compensation programs, and ensuring compliance with labor laws and regulations. In this article, we will discuss the importance of HRM, the key functions of HRM, and some of the challenges faced by HR managers.

Importance of HRM
HRM plays a critical role in the success of any organization. The following are some of the reasons why HRM is important:

Recruitment and retention: HRM is responsible for recruiting and selecting the best candidates for job openings, as well as retaining top talent through effective employee engagement strategies.

Training and development: HRM ensures that employees receive the necessary training and development to perform their jobs effectively and advance in their careers.

Compliance: HRM ensures that the organization complies with labor laws and regulations, including those related to equal employment opportunities, wage and hour laws, and workplace safety.

Compensation and benefits: HRM manages employee compensation and benefits programs, ensuring that employees are paid fairly and receive appropriate benefits.

Key Functions of HRM
Recruitment and selection: HRM is responsible for attracting, screening, and selecting qualified candidates for job openings.

Training and development: HRM designs and implements training programs that help employees develop the skills and knowledge they need to perform their jobs effectively and advance in their careers.

Performance management: HRM is responsible for evaluating employee performance and providing feedback and coaching to help employees improve.

Compensation and benefits: HRM designs and manages employee compensation and benefits programs, including salaries, bonuses, and health insurance.

Employee relations: HRM is responsible for managing employee relations, including addressing employee grievances, resolving conflicts, and promoting employee engagement.

Challenges Faced by HR Managers
HR managers face several challenges in managing employees, including the following:

Compliance with labor laws and regulations: HR managers must ensure that the organization complies with a complex set of labor laws and regulations, which can be challenging to navigate.

Managing diversity: HR managers must promote diversity and inclusion in the workplace, which requires sensitivity to cultural differences and effective communication skills.

Employee retention: HR managers must develop strategies to retain top talent and keep employees engaged and motivated.

Managing change: HR managers must be able to manage change effectively, including implementing new policies and procedures and responding to changes in the business environment.

In conclusion, HRM is a critical function in any organization. By managing employee recruitment, training and development, compensation and benefits, compliance, and employee relations, HR managers can help organizations achieve their goals and objectives. However, HR managers also face several challenges, including managing compliance with labor laws and regulations, promoting diversity and inclusion, retaining top talent, and managing change effectively.

Write about Attracting and retaining top talent Attracting and retaining top talent is essential for the success of any organization. Top talent refers to highly skilled and qualified individuals who can bring value to an organization and help it achieve its goals and objectives. In this article, we will discuss some strategies that organizations can use to attract and retain top talent.

Attracting Top Talent

Employer branding: Building a strong employer brand can help organizations attract top talent. This includes creating a positive image of the organization, highlighting its strengths and values, and promoting a positive work culture.

Referral programs: Offering referral bonuses to employees who refer top talent can be an effective way to attract highly qualified candidates.

Social media recruiting: Using social media platforms like LinkedIn, Facebook, and Twitter to promote job openings and connect with potential candidates can be an effective way to attract top talent.

Offering competitive compensation and benefits: Offering competitive compensation and benefits packages can make an organization more attractive to top talent.

Professional development opportunities: Offering professional development opportunities, such as training and mentoring programs, can attract top talent who value continuous learning and career advancement.

Retaining Top Talent
Providing a positive work environment: Creating a positive work environment that fosters collaboration, respect, and creativity can help retain top talent.

Offering competitive compensation and benefits: Offering competitive salaries, bonuses, and benefits can help retain top talent and prevent them from seeking opportunities elsewhere.

Career advancement opportunities: Providing career advancement opportunities, such as promotions and leadership training, can help retain top talent by giving them a clear path for growth and development within the organization.

Employee recognition programs: Recognizing and rewarding top performers can help retain top talent by showing them that their contributions are valued and appreciated.

Flexible work arrangements: Offering flexible work arrangements, such as remote work options and flexible schedules, can help retain top talent who value work-life balance.

In conclusion, attracting and retaining top talent is crucial for the success of any organization. By building a strong employer brand, offering competitive compensation and benefits, providing professional development opportunities, and creating a positive work environment, organizations can attract and retain top talent. However, organizations must also focus on retaining top talent by offering career advancement opportunities, employee recognition programs, and flexible work arrangements.

Developing An Employee Handbook And Providing Training And Development

opportunities are important aspects of human resources management. In this article, we will discuss the importance of an employee handbook, the key elements of an effective handbook, and the benefits of providing training and development opportunities.

Developing an Employee Handbook
An employee handbook is a document that outlines an organization's policies, procedures, and expectations for employees. An effective employee handbook is essential for communicating important information to employees, ensuring compliance with labor laws and regulations, and promoting a positive work culture. The following are key elements of an effective employee handbook:

Introduction: This section should include an overview of the organization's mission, values, and culture.

Employment policies: This section should include policies related to employment, such as equal employment opportunities, anti-discrimination policies, and workplace safety.

Code of conduct: This section should outline the organization's expectations for employee behavior, including guidelines for professional conduct, dress code, and use of technology.

Compensation and benefits: This section should include information about employee compensation, benefits, and leave policies.

Performance management: This section should outline the organization's performance management process, including employee evaluations, feedback, and development plans.

Providing Training and Development Opportunities

Training and development opportunities are essential for promoting employee growth and development, improving job performance, and retaining top talent. The following are some benefits of providing training and development opportunities:

Improved job performance: Training and development can help employees acquire new skills and knowledge that can improve their job performance.

Career advancement: Training and development can help employees develop the skills and knowledge they need to advance in their careers.

Increased job satisfaction: Providing training and development opportunities can improve employee satisfaction by showing that the organization values their growth and development.

Retention of top talent: Providing training and development opportunities can help retain top talent by providing opportunities for growth and development within the organization.

Improved organizational performance: Training and development can improve overall organizational performance by ensuring that employees have the skills and knowledge they need to perform their jobs effectively.

In conclusion, developing an employee handbook and providing training and development opportunities are important aspects of human resources management. An effective employee handbook can help communicate important information to employees, ensure compliance with labor laws and regulations, and promote a positive work culture. Providing training and development opportunities can promote employee growth and development, improve job performance, and help retain top talent.

CHAPTER SEVEN

INNOVATION AND ADAPTABILITY

Innovation and adaptability are two critical factors for success in today's fast-paced and ever-changing business environment. In this article, we will discuss the importance of innovation and adaptability, as well as some strategies for fostering innovation and adaptability in organizations.

Importance of Innovation
Innovation is the process of creating something new or improving upon existing products, services, or processes. In today's competitive business environment, innovation is essential for organizations to stay ahead of the curve and remain relevant to their customers. The following are some benefits of innovation:

Competitive advantage: Innovation can give organizations a competitive advantage by creating new products, services, or processes that set them apart from their competitors.

Increased efficiency: Innovation can lead to increased efficiency by streamlining processes and reducing costs.

Improved customer experience: Innovation can improve the customer experience by creating new products or services that better meet their needs.

Growth opportunities: Innovation can create new growth opportunities for organizations by expanding into new markets or industries.

Importance of Adaptability
Adaptability is the ability to adjust to changing circumstances and environments. In today's rapidly changing business environment, adaptability is essential for organizations to stay relevant and competitive. The following are some benefits of adaptability:

Flexibility: Adaptability allows organizations to be flexible and respond quickly to changes in the business environment.

Resilience: Adaptability helps organizations bounce back from setbacks and continue to thrive despite challenges.

Innovation: Adaptability fosters innovation by creating a culture of experimentation and learning.

Employee engagement: Adaptability can improve employee engagement by creating a culture of empowerment and collaboration.

Strategies for Fostering Innovation and Adaptability

Encourage experimentation: Encouraging experimentation can help foster innovation and adaptability by giving employees the freedom to explore new ideas and approaches.

Foster a culture of learning: Fostering a culture of learning can help employees stay up-to-date with the latest trends and technologies and adapt to changes in the business environment.

Promote collaboration: Promoting collaboration can help employees work together to solve problems and come up with innovative solutions.

Embrace technology: Embracing technology can help organizations stay ahead of the curve and adapt to changes in the business environment.

Stay customer-focused: Staying customer-focused can help organizations identify new opportunities for innovation and adapt to changes in customer needs and preferences.

In conclusion, innovation and adaptability are essential for organizations to stay ahead of the curve and remain relevant in today's fast-paced and ever-changing business environment. By fostering a culture of experimentation and learning, promoting collaboration, embracing technology, and staying customer-focused, organizations can foster innovation and adaptability and achieve long-term success.

Encouraging Creativity And Innovation
Encouraging creativity and innovation is essential for organizations to stay ahead of the curve and remain relevant in today's competitive business environment. In this article, we will discuss the importance of creativity and innovation, as well as some strategies for fostering creativity and innovation in organizations.

Importance Of Creativity And Innovation
Creativity and innovation are essential for organizations to remain competitive and adapt to changing market conditions. The following are some benefits of creativity and innovation:

Competitive advantage: Creativity and innovation can give organizations a competitive advantage by creating new products, services, or processes that set them apart from their competitors.

Increased efficiency: Creativity and innovation can lead to increased efficiency by streamlining processes and reducing costs.

Improved customer experience: Creativity and innovation can improve the customer experience by creating new products or services that better meet their needs.

Growth opportunities: Creativity and innovation can create new growth opportunities for organizations by expanding into new markets or industries.

Strategies for Fostering Creativity and Innovation

Encourage collaboration: Encouraging collaboration can help employees work together to solve problems and come up with innovative solutions.

Foster a culture of experimentation: Fostering a culture of experimentation can help employees feel empowered to try new things and explore new ideas.

Promote diversity and inclusion: Promoting diversity and inclusion can help organizations bring together people with different perspectives and ideas, which can lead to more creativity and innovation.

Provide resources and support: Providing resources and support, such as time, funding, and training, can help employees feel supported in their efforts to be creative and innovative.

Celebrate success: Celebrating success can help reinforce the importance of creativity and innovation and encourage employees to continue to think outside the box.

In conclusion, encouraging creativity and innovation is essential for organizations to stay ahead of the curve and remain relevant in today's competitive business environment. By encouraging collaboration, fostering a culture of experimentation, promoting diversity and inclusion, providing resources and support, and celebrating success, organizations can foster creativity and innovation and achieve long-term success.

Adopting new technologies and methods

Adopting new technologies and methods is essential for organizations to stay competitive and keep up with the rapidly evolving business landscape. In this article, we will discuss the importance of adopting new technologies and methods, as well as some strategies for successful adoption.

Importance of Adopting New Technologies and Methods

Adopting new technologies and methods can bring several benefits to organizations, including:

Improved efficiency: New technologies and methods can help organizations streamline processes, reduce costs, and improve productivity.

Increased competitiveness: Adopting new technologies and methods can help organizations stay ahead of the competition by offering better products or services, improving customer experiences, and reaching new markets.

Better decision-making: New technologies can provide better data analysis, which can lead to better decision-making and more informed business strategies.

Improved employee engagement: Adopting new technologies and methods can lead to better job satisfaction and improved employee engagement, as employees are able to work with the latest tools and techniques.

Strategies for Successful Adoption
Start with a plan: Before adopting new technologies or methods, it is important to have a clear plan in place that outlines the goals, timeline, and resources needed for successful adoption.

Involve key stakeholders: Involving key stakeholders, such as employees, customers, and partners, can help ensure successful adoption by gaining buy-in and feedback from those who will be impacted.

Provide training and support: Providing training and support can help employees learn new skills and feel confident in their ability to use new technologies and methods effectively.

Monitor and evaluate progress: Monitoring and evaluating progress can help organizations identify and address any issues or challenges that arise during the adoption process.

Be flexible and adaptable: Adopting new technologies and methods can be a complex process, so it is important to remain flexible and adaptable to changes in plans or unexpected challenges.

In conclusion, adopting new technologies and methods is essential for organizations to stay competitive and relevant in today's rapidly evolving business environment. By starting with a clear plan, involving key stakeholders, providing training and support, monitoring progress, and being flexible and adaptable, organizations can successfully adopt new technologies and methods and achieve long-term success.

REMAINING FLEXIBLE AND ADAPTABLE IN A CHANGING MARKET

Remaining flexible and adaptable in a changing market is essential for organizations to stay competitive and thrive in today's rapidly evolving business environment. In this article, we will discuss the importance of flexibility and adaptability, as well as some strategies for remaining flexible and adaptable.

IMPORTANCE OF FLEXIBILITY AND ADAPTABILITY

Flexibility and adaptability are essential for organizations to remain competitive in a changing market. The following are some benefits of flexibility and adaptability:

Ability to respond to changes: Flexibility and adaptability enable organizations to respond quickly and effectively to changes in the market, such as new competition, changing customer needs, or economic downturns.

Improved innovation: Flexibility and adaptability can lead to improved innovation by allowing organizations to experiment with new ideas and approaches.

Increased agility: Flexibility and adaptability can increase an organization's agility by enabling it to pivot quickly and efficiently when needed.

Better employee morale: Flexibility and adaptability can lead to better employee morale by allowing employees to work in an environment that values their input and encourages them to think creatively.

Strategies for Remaining Flexible and Adaptable

Embrace change: Embracing change and being open to new ideas and approaches can help organizations remain flexible and adaptable.

Foster a culture of innovation: Fostering a culture of innovation can encourage employees to think creatively and come up with new solutions to problems.

Monitor market trends: Monitoring market trends can help organizations anticipate changes and prepare for them in advance.

Build a diverse team: Building a diverse team with a range of skills and perspectives can help organizations adapt to changes in the market and respond to new challenges.

Continuously learn and improve: Continuously learning and improving can help organizations stay ahead of the curve and remain competitive in a changing market.

In conclusion, remaining flexible and adaptable in a changing market is essential for organizations to stay competitive and thrive. By embracing change, fostering a culture of innovation, monitoring market trends, building a diverse team, and continuously learning and improving, organizations can remain flexible and adaptable and achieve long-term success.

CHAPTER EIGHT

MARKETING AND BRANDING

Marketing and branding are two fundamental elements of any successful business strategy. Marketing refers to the activities a company undertakes to promote and sell its products or services, while branding encompasses the overall identity and perception of the company among consumers.

Marketing involves a range of activities, including market research, advertising, promotions, public relations, and sales. It is an essential component of any business as it helps to create awareness of products or services, generate demand, and ultimately drive sales.

Branding, on the other hand, is the process of creating a unique identity for a company or product that sets it apart from competitors. This identity encompasses everything from the name and logo to the company's values, mission, and personality. A strong brand can help establish credibility, build trust with customers, and create a loyal customer base.

Together, marketing and branding form the foundation of a company's overall strategy for success. Effective marketing and branding can help a company to stand out in a crowded marketplace, build strong customer relationships, and ultimately drive growth and profitability.

Creating A Strong Brand Identity

Creating a strong brand identity is essential for businesses looking to establish a unique and recognizable presence in the market. A strong brand identity helps to build trust with customers, differentiate the company from competitors, and create a sense of consistency and familiarity across all touchpoints. Here are some key strategies for creating a strong brand identity:

Define your brand's mission and values: Before creating a visual identity for your brand, it's important to define your brand's mission and values. What sets your brand apart from competitors? What values does your brand stand for? What problem does your brand solve for customers? Defining these core elements of your brand can help guide the development of your visual identity.

Develop a memorable logo: A logo is a key component of any brand identity. It should be simple, easily recognizable, and memorable. A good logo should also be versatile enough to be used across a range of mediums and sizes.

Choose a color palette: Colors play a significant role in brand identity. They can evoke emotions, communicate key messages, and differentiate the brand from competitors. When choosing a color palette, consider the personality and values of your brand, as well as the emotions you want to evoke in customers.

Establish a consistent visual style: Consistency is key when it comes to brand identity. Establishing a consistent visual style across all touchpoints, including packaging, advertising, and social media, can help to reinforce your brand's identity and make it more recognizable.

Develop a brand voice: Your brand voice is the tone and style of communication used to interact with customers. Whether it's serious and professional or playful and witty, your brand voice should be consistent across all channels and reflect the personality of your brand.

Create brand guidelines: Brand guidelines are a set of rules and guidelines that outline how your brand should be presented visually and verbally. They ensure consistency across all touchpoints and can be a valuable resource for employees and external partners.

Creating a strong brand identity takes time and effort, but the benefits are worth it. A strong brand identity can help to build trust with customers, differentiate your brand from competitors, and ultimately drive growth and profitability.

DEVELOPING A MARKETING PLAN AND EXECUTING IT EFFECTIVELY

Developing a marketing plan is essential for businesses looking to effectively promote their products or services and reach their target audience. Here are some key steps for developing a marketing plan and executing it effectively:

Define your target audience: The first step in developing a marketing plan is to define your target audience. Who are your ideal customers? What are their needs and pain points? Understanding your target audience is essential for developing messaging that resonates with them.

Set measurable goals: Once you've defined your target audience, it's important to set measurable goals for your marketing efforts. Whether it's increasing website traffic, generating leads, or driving sales, setting clear goals can help you track progress and measure success.

Develop a budget: Your marketing budget should be based on your overall business goals and the resources you have available. Consider allocating resources to a mix of tactics, including advertising, content marketing, social media, and email marketing.

Choose your tactics: Based on your target audience, goals, and budget, choose the marketing tactics that are most likely to be effective. Consider a mix of tactics, including paid advertising, content marketing, social media, and email marketing.

Develop a content strategy: Creating content that resonates with your target audience is an effective way to build brand awareness, establish credibility, and generate leads. Develop a content strategy that includes blog posts, social media posts, videos, and other types of content.

Measure and analyze results: It's important to measure and analyze the results of your marketing efforts to determine what's working and what's not. Use analytics tools to track website traffic, social media engagement, and other metrics, and make adjustments to your tactics as needed.

Executing a marketing plan effectively requires focus, discipline, and attention to detail. By following these steps and consistently executing your marketing plan, you can effectively promote your products or services, build brand awareness, and achieve your business goals.

DEVELOPING A MARKETING PLAN AND EXECUTING IT EFFECTIVELY

Developing a marketing plan is essential for businesses looking to effectively promote their products or services and reach their target audience. Here are some key steps for developing a marketing plan and executing it effectively:

Define your target audience: The first step in developing a marketing plan is to define your target audience. Who are your ideal customers? What are their needs and pain points? Understanding your target audience is essential for developing messaging that resonates with them.

Set measurable goals: Once you've defined your target audience, it's important to set measurable goals for your marketing efforts. Whether it's increasing website traffic, generating leads, or driving sales, setting clear goals can help you track progress and measure success.

Develop a budget: Your marketing budget should be based on your overall business goals and the resources you have available. Consider allocating resources to a mix of tactics, including advertising, content marketing, social media, and email marketing.

Choose your tactics: Based on your target audience, goals, and budget, choose the marketing tactics that are most likely to be effective. Consider a mix of tactics, including paid advertising, content marketing, social media, and email marketing.

Develop a content strategy: Creating content that resonates with your target audience is an effective way to build brand awareness, establish credibility, and generate leads. Develop a content strategy that includes blog posts, social media posts, videos, and other types of content.

Measure and analyze results: It's important to measure and analyze the results of your marketing efforts to determine what's working and what's not. Use analytics tools to track website traffic, social media engagement, and other metrics, and make adjustments to your tactics as needed.

Executing a marketing plan effectively requires focus, discipline, and attention to detail. By following these steps and consistently executing your marketing plan, you can effectively promote your products or services, build brand awareness, and achieve your business goals.

LEVERAGING SOCIAL MEDIA AND OTHER DIGITAL CHANNELS

Social media and digital channels have become a crucial part of the modern marketing mix, providing businesses with a cost-effective way to reach and engage with their target audience. Here are some key strategies for leveraging social media and other digital channels:

Define your social media goals: Before diving into social media, it's important to define your goals. What do you want to achieve through social media? Whether it's building brand awareness, generating leads, or driving sales, setting clear goals can help you develop a more effective social media strategy.

Choose the right platforms: There are numerous social media platforms to choose from, each with its own unique features and audience demographics. Choose the platforms that are most likely to be effective for reaching your target audience.

Develop a content strategy: Creating engaging and valuable content is essential for building a strong social media presence. Develop a content strategy that includes a mix of text, images, videos, and other types of content that resonate with your target audience.

Build a community: Social media is all about building relationships with your audience. Engage with your followers, respond to comments and messages, and foster a sense of community around your brand.

Use paid advertising: While organic reach on social media has declined in recent years, paid advertising can help you reach a wider audience and drive targeted traffic to your website or landing pages.

Monitor and measure results: Use analytics tools to track your social media performance and make adjustments to your strategy as needed. Monitor metrics such as engagement rates, follower growth, and website traffic to determine what's working and what's not.

In addition to social media, there are numerous other digital channels you can leverage to promote your business, including email marketing, search engine optimization (SEO), content marketing, and influencer marketing. By leveraging a mix of digital channels and consistently executing your strategy, you can effectively reach and engage with your target audience and achieve your business goals.

CHAPTER NINE

CUSTOMER RELATIONSHIP MANAGEMENT

Customer relationship management (CRM) is a strategy that businesses use to manage their interactions with customers and potential customers. The goal of CRM is to improve customer satisfaction and loyalty, while also driving sales and revenue growth. Here are some key elements of a CRM strategy:

Customer data management: To effectively manage customer relationships, businesses need to have a centralized database that contains customer data such as contact information, purchase history, and interactions with the company.

Sales automation: CRM software can automate the sales process by providing tools for managing leads, tracking sales activity, and managing the sales pipeline.

Marketing automation: CRM software can also help automate marketing activities such as email campaigns, social media marketing, and targeted advertising.

Customer service and support: CRM software can help businesses provide better customer service by tracking customer inquiries and support requests and ensuring timely follow-up.

Analytics and reporting: By analyzing customer data, businesses can gain insights into customer behavior and preferences, which can inform marketing and sales strategies.

Personalization: CRM software can help businesses personalize their interactions with customers by providing data on past purchases and preferences, allowing for more tailored marketing and sales efforts.

Effective CRM requires a customer-centric approach and a commitment to providing a positive customer experience. By leveraging CRM software and best practices, businesses can improve customer satisfaction, increase customer loyalty, and drive revenue growth.

PROVIDING EXCELLENT CUSTOMER SERVICE

Providing excellent customer service is a crucial element of building a strong brand and fostering customer loyalty. Here are some key strategies for providing excellent customer service:

Respond promptly: Whether it's a phone call, email, or social media message, respond to customer inquiries as quickly as possible. This shows that you value their time and are committed to addressing their needs.

Listen actively: When interacting with customers, actively listen to their concerns and needs. Ask questions to clarify their needs and show empathy for their situation.

Be proactive: Anticipate customer needs and proactively offer solutions or assistance. This can help prevent issues from arising and demonstrate your commitment to customer satisfaction.

Personalize interactions: Use customer data to personalize interactions and make customers feel valued. Address them by name, reference their past purchases, and offer tailored recommendations.

Follow up: After resolving an issue or completing a sale, follow up with customers to ensure their satisfaction and offer additional assistance if needed.

Empower employees: Give employees the tools and autonomy to resolve customer issues and provide exceptional service. Empowered employees are more likely to go above and beyond for customers.

Providing excellent customer service requires a customer-centric approach and a commitment to continuous improvement. By listening to customer feedback, analyzing customer data, and consistently delivering exceptional service, businesses can build a loyal customer base and differentiate themselves from competitors.

BUILDING STRONG RELATIONSHIPS WITH CUSTOMERS

Building strong relationships with customers is essential for creating loyalty and driving long-term success. Here are some key strategies for building strong relationships with customers:

Consistent communication: Regularly communicate with customers through a variety of channels, such as email, social media, and phone calls. This can help keep your brand top-of-mind and demonstrate your commitment to customer satisfaction.

Personalization: Use customer data to personalize interactions and make customers feel valued. Address them by name, reference their past purchases, and offer tailored recommendations.

Timely follow-up: Follow up with customers after sales or interactions to ensure their satisfaction and offer additional assistance if needed. Timely follow-up shows that you care about their experience and are committed to providing ongoing support.

Exceptional customer service: Provide exceptional customer service by responding quickly to inquiries, actively listening to customer needs, and proactively addressing issues.

Customer feedback: Collect and analyze customer feedback to identify areas for improvement and demonstrate that you value their opinions.

Loyalty programs: Offer loyalty programs or rewards to incentivize repeat purchases and show appreciation for customer loyalty.

Community building: Foster a sense of community among customers by creating forums, groups, or events where customers can connect with each other and your brand.

Building strong relationships with customers requires a customer-centric approach and a commitment to ongoing engagement. By consistently delivering exceptional service, personalizing interactions, and fostering a sense of community, businesses can build loyal customers who advocate for their brand and drive long-term **success.**

CUSTOMER FEEDBACK TO IMPROVE PRODUCTS AND SERVICES

Using customer feedback is essential for improving products and services and ensuring that they meet customer needs and expectations.

Here are some key strategies for using customer feedback to improve products and services:

Collect feedback: Collect feedback from customers through surveys, social media, customer support interactions, and other channels. Make sure to ask open-ended questions that encourage detailed responses.

Analyze feedback: Analyze feedback to identify trends, patterns, and areas for improvement. Look for common themes or issues that arise across multiple feedback channels.

Prioritize changes: Prioritize changes based on the impact they will have on customer satisfaction and the resources required to implement them.

Communicate changes: Communicate changes to customers through email, social media, or other channels to show that you are committed to addressing their feedback and improving their experience.

Test changes: Test changes before implementing them on a large scale to ensure they have the desired impact and don't create new issues.

Continuously monitor feedback: Continuously monitor feedback to ensure that changes have the desired impact and to identify new areas for improvement.

Using customer feedback to improve products and services requires a customer-centric approach and a commitment to continuous improvement. By collecting and analyzing feedback, prioritizing changes, testing changes, and communicating with customers, businesses can ensure that their products and services meet customer needs and expectations and drive long-term success.

CHAPTER TEN

COMMUNITY INVOLVEMENT AND CORPORATE SOCIAL RESPONSIBILITY

Community involvement and corporate social responsibility (CSR) are important components of building a positive reputation and demonstrating a commitment to making a positive impact on society. Here are some key strategies for community involvement and CSR:

Identify community needs: Identify the needs of the community and causes that align with your business values and mission. This can be done through research, community outreach, and engagement with stakeholders.

Volunteerism: Encourage employees to volunteer their time and skills to support local organizations and causes. This can help build strong relationships with the community and demonstrate a commitment to making a positive impact.

Sponsorship: Sponsor local events, fundraisers, and organizations to build brand visibility and demonstrate a commitment to the community.

Sustainable business practices: Implement sustainable business practices, such as reducing waste, conserving energy, and using environmentally friendly products. This can help reduce your environmental footprint and demonstrate a commitment to sustainability.

Philanthropy: Donate a portion of profits or resources to support local organizations and causes. This can help build goodwill and demonstrate a commitment to giving back.

Ethical business practices: Implement ethical business practices, such as fair labor practices and transparency in supply chain management. This can help build trust with customers and demonstrate a commitment to doing business in a responsible manner.

Community involvement and CSR are important for building a positive reputation and demonstrating a commitment to making a positive impact on society. By identifying community needs, encouraging volunteerism, sponsoring local events, implementing sustainable and ethical business practices, and donating resources to support local causes, businesses can build strong relationships with the community and drive long-term success.

Contributing to the local community and Supporting social and environmental causes

Contributing to the local community and supporting social and environmental causes are important ways for businesses to make a positive impact on society and build a positive reputation. Here are some key strategies for contributing to the local community and supporting social and environmental causes:

Volunteerism: Encourage employees to volunteer their time and skills to support local organizations and causes. This can help build strong relationships with the community and demonstrate a commitment to making a positive impact.

Sponsorship: Sponsor local events, fundraisers, and organizations to build brand visibility and demonstrate a commitment to the community. This can help raise awareness for important social and environmental causes.

Donations: Donate a portion of profits or resources to support local organizations and causes. This can help build goodwill and demonstrate a commitment to giving back.

Environmental sustainability: Implement sustainable business practices, such as reducing waste, conserving energy, and using environmentally friendly products. This can help reduce your environmental footprint and demonstrate a commitment to sustainability.

Ethical business practices: Implement ethical business practices, such as fair labor practices and transparency in supply chain management. This can help build trust with customers and demonstrate a commitment to doing business in a responsible manner.

Partnerships: Partner with local organizations and causes to build a collaborative approach to solving social and environmental issues. This can help build strong relationships with the community and drive positive change.

Contributing to the local community and supporting social and environmental causes can help businesses build a positive reputation, attract socially conscious customers, and drive long-term success. By encouraging volunteerism, sponsoring local events, donating resources, implementing sustainable and ethical business practices, and building partnerships with local organizations and causes, businesses can make a positive impact on society and the environment.

ENCOURAGING EMPLOYEES TO VOLUNTEER AND PARTICIPATE IN CHARITABLE INITIATIVES

Encouraging employees to volunteer and participate in charitable initiatives is a great way for businesses to contribute to the community and build a positive reputation. Here are some strategies for encouraging employees to get involved:

Provide paid volunteer time off: Offer paid time off for employees to volunteer with a nonprofit organization or charitable cause. This can help employees feel more connected to the community and demonstrate a commitment to giving back.

Create a volunteer program: Create a formal volunteer program that encourages employees to get involved in local charities or nonprofit organizations. This can include organizing volunteer events, such as community service days or fundraising activities.

Match employee donations: Offer to match employee donations to charitable causes, which can encourage employees to donate more and demonstrate a commitment to making a positive impact.

Recognize employee contributions: Recognize and reward employees who make significant contributions to charitable causes. This can include acknowledging their efforts in company-wide communications, offering public recognition, or providing additional time off.

Provide opportunities for skill-based volunteering: Offer opportunities for employees to use their professional skills to support nonprofit organizations or charitable causes.

This can help employees feel more engaged and motivated while making a positive impact.

Encouraging employees to volunteer and participate in charitable initiatives can help build a positive corporate culture, improve employee morale and engagement, and demonstrate a commitment to making a positive impact on society. By providing paid volunteer time off, creating a formal volunteer program, matching employee donations, recognizing employee contributions, and providing opportunities for skill-based volunteering, businesses can inspire their employees to get involved and make a difference in the community.

www.ingramcontent.com/pod-product-compliance
Lightning Source LLC
Chambersburg PA
CBHW071137220526
45467CB00015B/1278